EXPERIENCING CHRISTMAS

LEADER GUIDE

Experiencing Christmas:
Christ in the Sights and Sounds of Advent

Experiencing Christmas
978-1-7910-2927-2
978-1-7910-2928-9 *eBook*

Experiencing Christmas: Leader Guide
978-1-7910-2929-6
978-1-7910-2930-2 *eBook*

Experiencing Christmas: DVD
978-1-7910-2931-9

Download a FREE children's leader guide
and youth study at
abingdonpress.com/experiencingchristmas.

Also by Matt Rawle

The Faith of a Mockingbird

The Redemption of Scrooge

What Makes a Hero?

The Gift of the Nutcracker

The Grace of Les Miserables

The Heart that Grew Three Sizes

Jesus Revealed

For more information, visit MattRawle.com.

MATT RAWLE

EXPERIENCING CHRISTMAS

CHRIST IN THE SIGHTS AND SOUNDS OF ADVENT

LEADER GUIDE

Abingdon Press | Nashville

Experiencing Christmas
Christ in the Sights and Sounds of Advent
Leader Guide

978-1-7910-2929-6

MANUFACTURED IN THE UNITED STATES OF AMERICA

CONTENTS

ABOUT THE
LEADER GUIDE WRITER

Sally Sharpe is a certified spiritual director who is passionate about companioning others on the spiritual journey, helping to guide them toward greater healing and wholeness. Believing that all people long to be seen, known, and loved, she provides a safe space for others to share their stories, explore their relationship with God, and seek a deeper connection with the One who knows them best and loves them most. Areas of special interest include journaling, storytelling for healing, Ignatian spirituality/spiritual discernment, contemplative prayer practices, the Enneagram, and inner healing (Internal Family Systems and HeartSync prayer).

Formerly, Sally was senior editor of Abingdon Women (published by Abingdon Press), a line of in-depth Bible studies that she created and helped to grow into a thriving line. During her many years in Christian publishing, Sally also edited a line of Christian living books and devotionals, as well as books for clergy and church leadership. Combining her skills in content development/writing, interpersonal connection, and spiritual formation, she enjoys creating experiences and resources that help others draw closer to God and become the persons God created them to be. Sally and Neil have two young adult daughters and live just outside of Nashville in Mt. Juliet, Tennessee.

TO THE LEADER

We experience the world through our senses—what we can see, hear, touch, smell, and taste. And at Christmas, our senses are *saturated* with stimuli—lovely visuals, beautiful music, delightful textures, fragrant holiday scents, and delicious food. It is a time when we celebrate that God, who came from heaven to earth, knows what it is like to experience the world as we do. God now has senses—eyes to see suffering and ears to hear lament, knowing the saltiness of tears and the desire for compassionate touch. In the person of Jesus, God put on flesh and all that comes with it—growing pains, thirsting after a long day's journey, the joy of an early morning stretch, tired feet, sunburned skin, and even the suffering of crucifixion. God did this not to experience humanity and then let us be. God entered into our story so that our story might be redeemed!

In *Experiencing Christmas: Christ in the Sights and Sounds of Advent*, author and pastor Matt Rawle invites us to rediscover the meaning of the Advent season as we experience Christmas with all our senses. In each chapter, we'll consider one of our senses and its unique encounters during Advent—things we see, hear, taste (and smell), and touch— with a final word about our call to be the aroma of Christ in all we do. We'll discover how our senses become signs for us, pointing to the Incarnation when God took on human flesh and experienced the world as we do so that we might taste the goodness of God.

How to Facilitate This Study

This four-session study makes use of the following components:

- the study book, *Experiencing Christmas: Christ in the Sights and Sounds of Advent* by Matt Rawle
- this Leader Guide
- *Experiencing Christmas: Christ in the Sights and Sounds of Advent* DVD or a subscription to Amplify Media to access the streaming videos (www.amplifymedia.com)

You will need a DVD player or computer and a television or projection screen so that you can watch the DVD segments as part of your group session. If you or your church has a subscription to Amplify Media, use your login and find the videos by searching for *Experiencing Christmas*. Participants in the study will need access to Bibles during the session; you also might want to have on hand basic supplies such as a markerboard or large sheets of paper and markers for recording group members' responses, and pens and paper for note taking, if desired.

Each session is structured into a 60-minute format and includes the following sections:

- Planning the Session (contains session objectives, biblical foundation passages, and preparation steps to take)
- Opening Activity and Prayer (5 minutes)
- Watch DVD Segment (10 minutes)
- Study and Discussion (35-40 minutes)
- Closing Activity and Prayer (5 minutes)

If you have more time in your session, or want to utilize more activities during your session, "Additional Options for Group Activity" are included, listed after the closing prayer.

HELPFUL HINTS

Preparing for Each Session

- Pray for wisdom and discernment from the Holy Spirit, for you and for each member of the group, as you prepare for the study.
- Before each session, familiarize yourself with the content. Read the study book chapter again.
- Choose the session elements you will use during the group session, including the specific discussion questions you plan to cover. Be prepared, however, to adjust the session as group members interact and questions arise. Prepare carefully, but allow space for the Holy Spirit to move in and through the group members and through you as facilitator.
- Prepare the space where the group will meet so that the space will enhance the learning process. Ideally, group members should be seated around a table or in a circle so that all can see one another. Movable chairs are best so that the group easily can form pairs or small teams for discussion.

Shaping the Learning Environment

- Create a climate of openness, encouraging group members to participate as they feel comfortable.
- Remember that some people will jump right in with answers and comments, while others need time to process what is being discussed.
- If you notice that some group members seem never to be able to enter the conversation, ask them if they have thoughts to

share. Give everyone a chance to talk, but keep the conversation moving. Moderate to prevent a few individuals from doing all the talking.

- Communicate the importance of group discussions and group exercises.
- If no one answers at first during discussions, do not be afraid of silence. Count silently to ten, then say something such as, "Would anyone like to go first?" If no one responds, venture an answer yourself and ask for comments.
- Model openness as you share with the group. Group members will follow your example. If you limit your sharing to a surface level, others will follow suit.
- Encourage multiple answers or responses before moving on to the next question.
- Ask: "Why?" or "Why do you believe that?" or "Can you say more about that?" to help continue a discussion and give it greater depth.
- Affirm others' responses with comments such as "Great" or "Thanks" or "Good insight"—especially if it's the first time someone has spoken during the group session.
- Monitor your own contributions. If you are doing most of the talking, back off so that you do not train the group to listen rather than speak up.
- Remember that you do not have to have all the answers. Your job is to keep the discussion going and encourage participation.

Managing the Session

- Honor the time schedule. If a session is running longer than expected, get consensus from the group before continuing beyond the agreed-upon ending time.
- Involve group members in various aspects of the group session, such as saying prayers or reading the Scripture.

- Note that the session guides sometimes call for breaking into smaller groups or pairs. This gives everyone a chance to speak and participate fully. Mix up the groups; don't let the same people pair up for every activity.
- As always in discussions that may involve personal sharing, confidentiality is essential. Group members should never pass along stories that have been shared in the group. Remind the group members at each session: confidentiality is crucial to the success of this study.

Adapting for Virtual Small Group Sessions

Meeting online is a great option for a number of situations. During a time of a public-health hazard, such as the COVID-19 pandemic, online meetings are a welcome opportunity for people to converse while seeing each other's faces. Online meetings can also expand the "neighborhood" of possible group members because people can log in from just about anywhere in the world. This also gives those who do not have access to transportation or who prefer not to travel at certain times of day the chance to participate.

The following guidelines will help you lead an effective and enriching group study using an online video conferencing platform such as Zoom, Webex, Google Meet, Microsoft Teams, or another virtual meeting platform of your choice.

Tips for Online Meetings

When circumstances preclude meeting in person, online meetings are a welcome opportunity for people to converse while seeing each other's faces. Online meetings can also expand the "neighborhood" of possible group members because people can log in from just about anywhere in the world. This also gives those who do not have access to transportation or who prefer not to travel at certain times of day the chance to participate.

One popular option is Zoom. This platform is used quite a bit by businesses. If your church has an account, this can be a good medium. Google Meet, Webex, and Microsoft Teams are other good choices. Individuals can obtain free accounts for each of these platforms, but there may be restrictions (for instance, Zoom's free version limits meetings to 40 minutes). Check each platform's website to be sure you are aware of any such restrictions before you sign up.

Video Sharing

For a video-based study, it's important to be able to screen-share your videos so that all participants can view them in your study session. The good news is, whether you have the videos on DVD or streaming files, it is possible to play them in your session.

- All of the videoconferencing platforms mentioned previously support screen-sharing videos. Some have specific requirements for assuring that sound will play clearly in addition to the videos. Follow your videoconferencing platform instructions carefully, and test the video sharing in advance to be sure it works.

- If you wish to screen-share a DVD video, you may need to use a different media player. Some media players will not allow you to share your screen when you play copyright-protected DVDs. VLC is a free media player that is safe and easy to use. To try this software, download at videolan .org/VLC.

- *What about copyright?* DVDs like those you use for group study are meant to be used in a group setting in "real time." That is, whether you meet in person, online, or in a hybrid setting, Abingdon Press encourages use of your DVD or streaming video.

- *What is allowed:* Streaming an Abingdon DVD over Zoom, Teams, or a similar platform during a small group session.

- *What is not allowed:* Posting video of a published DVD study to social media or YouTube for later viewing.

- If you have any questions about permissions and copyright, email permissions@abingdonpress.com.

- The streaming subscription platform Amplify Media makes it easy to share streaming videos for groups. When your church has an Amplify subscription, your group members can sign on and have access to the video sessions.

- Visit AmplifyMedia.com to learn more.

Training and Practice

- Choose a platform and practice using it so you are comfortable with it. Engage in a couple of practice runs with another person.

- Set up a training meeting.

- In advance, teach participants how to log in. Tell them that you will send them an invitation via email, and that it will include a link for them to click at the time of the meeting.

- For those who do not have internet service, let them know they may telephone into the meeting. Provide them the number and let them know that there is usually a unique phone number for each meeting.

- During the training meeting, show them the basic tools available for them to use. They can learn other tools as they feel more confident.

During the Meetings

- **Early invitations.** Send out invitations at least a week in advance. Many meeting platforms enable you to do this through their software.

- **Early log in.** Participants should log in at least ten minutes in advance to test their audio and video connections.

- **Talking/not talking.** Instruct participants to keep their microphones muted during the meeting, so extraneous noise from their location does not interrupt the meeting. This includes chewing or yawning sounds, which can be embarrassing! When it is time for discussion, participants can unmute themselves. However, ask them to raise their hand or wave when they are ready to share so you can call on them. Give folks a few minutes to speak up. They may not be used to conversing in web conferences.

SESSION 1

DO YOU SEE WHAT I SEE?

PLANNING THE SESSION

Session Goals

Through this session's discussion and activities, participants will be encouraged to:

- Understand why it is incomplete to think of Advent as a time of anticipation.
- Consider how the lights and other visuals of Advent prepare us for something new and serve as deep symbols of hope.
- Learn the difference between anticipation and expectation.
- Explore how our imagination can help us with expectation and change our vision in Advent.

15

Biblical Foundation

- Luke 2:1
- Jeremiah 33:14-16
- Psalm 30:5
- Isaiah 40:3-4
- Isaiah 7:14
- Isaiah 9:6
- Luke 2:12, 29-32

Preparation

- Read the introduction and chapter 1, "Do You See What I See?" in Matt Rawle's *Experiencing Christmas*.
- Read through this Leader Guide session in its entirety to familiarize yourself with the material being covered.
- Read and reflect on this session's Biblical Foundation passages.
- Plan to have extra Bibles on hand for participants.
- You will want to have your DVD player or computer ready to watch the video segment.
- You also might have a markerboard or large sheet of paper available for recording group members' ideas and paper and pens for note taking, if desired.
- Have an Advent wreath, candles, and lighter available for the Closing Activity.
- If you will be doing the activities under "Additional Options for Group Activity," read through those options thoroughly and gather any items needed for that time together.

OPENING ACTIVITY AND PRAYER

Welcome participants as they arrive. When most are present, ask each group member to respond briefly to the following question, writing responses on a markerboard or large sheet of paper, if desired.

- What is a favorite Advent or Christmas experience, and which of your senses is most stimulated or utilized in this experience? (For example, the sound of a special song, the taste of a favorite dish, the smell of a Christmas tree, the feel of a warm mug of cocoa, and so on.)

Read aloud or summarize for the group:

These experiences we've shared, taken separately or together as a season of senses, are what it means to experience Christmas. The sights, sounds, smells, and tastes are different during the holidays. Christmas is so tied to our collective memory because it is so intimately connected to our senses. In Jesus, God entered into this world with eyes of God's own, so that we might see God's love clearly. Today we will be exploring how our sense of sight can enrich our experience and understanding of God's love this Christmas. Let's open in prayer.

Opening Prayer

God, thank you for this time together to gaze upon your Word. We pray that during this season of Advent you would enrich our experience of Christmas so that we might rediscover the meaning of the season. May our sense of sight become a sign for us, pointing us to the Incarnation so that we might experience your love in a new way today. We long to see your goodness; in Jesus's name. Amen.

WATCH DVD SEGMENT

Play session 1: "Do You See What I See?" on the *Experiencing Christmas* DVD or via Amplify Media.

Discuss:

- Did anything specific stand out as you watched the video?
- What is something you learned or experienced that seems new or *renewed*?

Invite the group to keep both the video and the book in mind throughout the discussion.

STUDY AND DISCUSSION

A Distant Glow

Read aloud or summarize for the group:

> Lights are one of the first signs that Christmas is near. Maybe more accurately, a lack of light begins to signal the changing seasons. At least for those of us north of the equator, the days begin to grow short.... For many, these short days offer an anxious anticipation for the next sunrise.... For others the darkness is no problem.... Whether you experience anxiety or you are filled with excitement...we all seem to agree that when it gets dark, we need more light. Either the light brings peace to the anxious heart or light offers beauty to those looking for some Christmas cheer. The light signals to us that something is different.
>
> There are other visual signs too.... There are reindeer in lawns, wreaths on streetlights, pop-up Christmas tree stands, inflatable Santas, and Salvation Army kettles in front of grocery stores. You don't have to be a Christian or a person of any faith tradition to recognize that change is in the air. You can see it with your own eyes.

- What are the sights that, for you, signal Christmas is coming?
- How do you respond to shorter days and more darkness? Do you experience anxiety, excitement, or something else?
- How do the lights of the Christmas season help to bring you peace or offer you beauty?

Read aloud or summarize for the group:

Advent is a season of anticipation. "This is a sign for you," the angels tell the shepherds as they were "guarding their sheep at night." This is something you need to see. This is something to look for.... We almost seem hardwired for anticipation, to recognize that we live in a world of cause and effect. The relationship between what we see and how we respond is basic to our human condition. Sight is a powerful sense. More than 50 percent of our brain's cortex, the outer layer of our brain, is dedicated to sight.[1]

- How does knowing that more than 50 percent of your brain's cortex is dedicated to sight affect your understanding of the importance of what you see?
- How would you define or explain *anticipation*?
- What does it mean to say that Advent is a season of anticipation?
- How do the sights of the season enrich your anticipation of Christmas and all that it means?

Read aloud or summarize for the group:

At the beginning of the Advent season, we dive into the prophetic poetry of the Hebrew Scriptures that our faith tradition has taught are signs for the coming Messiah. Jeremiah writes,

The time is coming, declares the LORD, when I will fulfill my gracious promise with the people of Israel and Judah. In those days and at that time, I will raise up a righteous branch from David's line, who will do what is just and right in the land. In those days, Judah will be saved and Jerusalem will live in safety. And this is what he will be called: The LORD Is Our Righteousness.

(Jeremiah 33:14-16 CEB)

---

1   Susan Hagen, "The Mind's Eye," *Rochester Review*, Vol. 74, No. 4, March-April 2012. Rochester.edu/pr/Review/V74N4/0402_brainscience.html (accessed May 4, 2023).

During the time that Jeremiah wrote his prophecy, Jerusalem was conquered by Babylon. Yet the prophet articulates hope that even in the midst of destruction, God is doing something wonderful. There's more to Advent than waiting in anticipation. There is hope.

- How do you imagine the people of Jeremiah's time received his words of hope?
- Who has offered you a vision of hope when all you could see was devastation?
- How do you desire to see and experience hope this Advent? What might help you in this?

The Holly and the Ivy

Read aloud or summarize for the group:

> Advent is full of visual markers of the season that represent something new is about to happen. But the decorations represent more than the coming of a new season. In a very real sense, these symbols mark the crucial transition between anticipation and expectation.

- Why is it incomplete to think of Advent as a season of anticipation?
- What are some of the markers of the season, and how do they serve as "deep symbols" of hope?
- How might you make room for hope this Advent? How might your anticipation become expectation?

From Anticipation to Expectation

Read aloud or summarize for the group:

> The journey from anticipation to expectation hinges on hope. Anticipation is based on what is known. Expectation never is. Anticipation is the fruit of previous knowledge, skill, and deduction, and its goal is an appropriate course

of action for what is coming. Conversely, you can't actively prepare for expectation. The only way to "prepare" for expectation is through imagination. The hope found within expectation is the acceptance of unfettered possibility.

- What are you anticipating about tomorrow? What are you expecting to happen? What's the difference?
- How would you define or describe the difference between anticipation and expectation in your life story?
- If the only way to prepare for expectation is through imagination, how might you open your imagination to what you've never before seen? How might expectation help you to change your vision in this Advent season?
- Discuss the metaphor of the "spiritual walk as a story in three chapters" with a "God box" that is taken apart and rebuilt until there is no longer a box (see pages 22–24 in *Experiencing Christmas*). What about this metaphor resonates with you, and what doesn't? Why?

CLOSING ACTIVITY AND PRAYER

Each week of our study, you will end the session by lighting candles on an Advent wreath and reading aloud Luke's account of the Christmas story, focusing your attention on one of the five senses.

Turn off the overhead lights and ask a group member to light the first Advent candle as participants watch in silence. Then have participants close their eyes and listen as you read the Scripture aloud slowly. Invite them to enter into the story using their imagination, becoming a participant in the scene and focusing primarily on *what they see*. Explain that using our God-given gift of imagination in this way brings the Scripture alive for us so that we may actually encounter God and experience God's goodness and love, not just know about

God. Begin with a prayer, asking God to give each of you the grace to see, trusting that the Holy Spirit is leading your imagination.

Read the account *slowly*, allowing brief pauses where indicated:

> *In those days a decree went out from Caesar Augustus that all the world should be registered. This was the first registration and was taken while Quirinius was governor of Syria. All went to their own towns to be registered. Joseph also went from the town of Nazareth in Galilee to Judea, to the city of David called Bethlehem, because he was descended from the house and family of David. He went to be registered with Mary, to whom he was engaged and who was expecting a child.*
>
> *(Luke 2:1-5)*

Say: *Notice what you see as you enter into this part of the story.* (Pause about 15 seconds.)

> *While they were there, the time came for her to deliver her child. And she gave birth to her firstborn son and wrapped him in bands of cloth and laid him in a manger, because there was no place in the guest room.*
>
> *(Luke 2:6-7)*

Say: *Notice what you see as you enter into this part of the story.* (Pause about 15 seconds.)

> *Now in that same region there were shepherds living in the fields, keeping watch over their flock by night. Then an angel of the Lord stood before them, and the glory of the Lord shone around them, and they were terrified. But the angel said to them, "Do not be afraid, for see, I am bringing you good news of great joy for all the people: to you is born this day in the city of David a Savior, who is the Messiah, the Lord. This will be a sign for you: you will find a child wrapped in bands of cloth and lying in a manger." And suddenly there was with the angel a multitude of the heavenly host, praising God and saying,*

"Glory to God in the highest heaven,
and on earth peace among those whom he favors!"
(Luke 2:8-14)

Say: *Notice what you see as you enter into this part of the story.* (Pause about 15 seconds.)

> *When the angels had left them and gone into heaven, the shepherds said to one another, "Let us go now to Bethlehem and see this thing that has taken place, which the Lord has made known to us." So they went with haste and found Mary and Joseph and the child lying in the manger. When they saw this, they made known what had been told them about this child, and all who heard it were amazed at what the shepherds told them, and Mary treasured all these words and pondered them in her heart.*
> (Luke 2:15-19)

Say: *Notice what you see as you enter into this part of the story.* (Pause about 15 seconds.)

> *The shepherds returned, glorifying and praising God for all they had heard and seen, just as it had been told them.*
> (Luke 2:20)

Say: *Notice what you see as you enter into this part of the story.* (Pause about 15 seconds.)

Invite participants to slowly return to the room and open their eyes when they are ready. Then move into a time of discussion.

Discuss:

• What did you notice as you entered the story, focusing on *what you saw*? What stood out to you and why?

Closing Prayer

God, you put on flesh and entered creation with eyes of your own, so that we might see your love clearly. As we gaze upon the symbols of the season,

23

remind us that the decorations represent more than the coming of a new season, more even than the coming of a child. They are symbols of the great hope we have in and through you. Open our eyes and fill us with expectant hope this Advent! Amen.

ADDITIONAL OPTIONS FOR GROUP ACTIVITIES

If your group is able to meet for longer than 60 minutes, consider adding one of the following activities that invite participants to experience the meaning of the season through their *sight*:

- **Share a favorite Christmas decoration**—In advance, invite each participant to bring a favorite Christmas decoration. Have group members take turns showing their items and telling why they are meaningful and how they serve as symbols of hope.

- **Decorate a Christmas tree**—Work together to decorate a Christmas tree for your meeting space. In advance, ask if anyone has an extra artificial tree they are not using and have group members bring lights and decorations. (If desired, have each person bring a favorite ornament and share the story of that ornament.) Or, if you would like to have a chrismon tree, search for chrismon patterns online and assemble the items needed to make them in advance. Then invite everyone to make an ornament at the end of the session. *(Note: If you have difficulty securing a tree, you could create a flat tree and flat ornaments using butcher or craft paper and display it on a wall.*

SESSION TWO

DO YOU HEAR
WHAT I HEAR?

PLANNING THE SESSION

Session Goals

Through this session's discussion and activities, participants will be encouraged to:

- Consider how music and other sounds enrich our experience of Christmas.
- Explore how music brings us together in ways that sometimes words can't.
- Discover how *verbal* praise is an integral part of the Christmas story, as well as the rest of Christ's story.
- Acknowledge that sometimes Christmas can be too loud and we need times of silence to ponder what God is doing around us and within us.

25

- Explore how to hold the tension of awe and anguish.

Biblical Foundation

- Isaiah 42:9-10
- Luke 2:13-14a
- Luke 2:19-20
- Luke 2:29-32
- Luke 19:37-38
- Luke 24:52-53

Preparation

- Read chapter 2, "Do You Hear What I Hear?" in Matt Rawle's *Experiencing Christmas*.
- Read through this Leader Guide session in its entirety to familiarize yourself with the material being covered.
- Read and reflect on the Biblical Foundation passages listed above.
- Plan to have extra Bibles on hand for participants.
- You will want to have your DVD player or computer ready to watch the video segment.
- You also might have a markerboard or large sheet of paper available for recording group members' ideas and paper and pens for note taking, if desired.
- Have an Advent wreath, candles, and lighter available for the Closing Activity, along with instrumental Christmas music.
- If you will be doing the activities under "Additional Options for Group Activity," read through those options thoroughly and gather any items needed for that time together.

OPENING ACTIVITY AND PRAYER

Welcome participants as they arrive. When most are present, ask each group member to respond briefly to the following question, writing responses on a markerboard or large sheet of paper, if desired.

- What is your favorite Christmas song and why?

Read aloud or summarize for the group:

> It seems impossible to imagine Christmas without music.
> But the soundtrack of the first Christmas included a variety
> of other sounds—perhaps bleating sheep, angels' voices,
> a baby's cry, and even silence. Today we will be explor-
> ing how the sounds of Christmas—then and now—can
> enrich our experience and understanding of God love's this
> Christmas. Let's open in prayer.

Opening Prayer

*God, thank you for this time together to listen to your Word. We pray
that during this season of Advent you would continue to enrich our
experience of Christmas so that we might rediscover the meaning of the
season. May our sense of hearing become a sign for us, pointing us to the
Incarnation so that we might experience your love in a new way today.
We long to hear your goodness; in Jesus's name. Amen.*

WATCH DVD SEGMENT

Play session 2: "Do You Hear What I Hear?" on the *Experiencing
Christmas* DVD or via Amplify Media.

Discuss:

- Did anything specific stand out as you watched the video?
- What is something you learned or experienced that seems new
  or *renewed*?

Invite the group to keep both the video and the book in mind
throughout the discussion.

STUDY AND DISCUSSION

Did You Hear That?

Read aloud or summarize for the group:

It seems impossible to imagine Christmas without music. What we hear shapes our experiences and our emotional memories. On the largest scale, music reveals that we might share more in common than we might imagine. Christmas music in particular brings us together in a way that sometimes words just can't.

- How do you imagine that first Christmas sounded? What story could be heard in addition to what our eyes might see?
- How does Christmas music shape your experience of Christmas? What other sounds of the season do you enjoy and why?
- How does Christmas music help you to feel connected to others—to your family, your faith community, and the larger body of Christ? What are some of the musical traditions of your faith community during Advent?

How Do You Say "Poinsettia" Anyway?

Read aloud or summarize for the group:

Speech, more so than music, grabs our attention in the Christmas story. I'd love to tell you that the angel of the Lord appeared before shepherds with a multitude of instruments filling the night sky with a magnificent "Gloria" in "Hark the Herald Angels Sing," but sadly there's no music in the story. "Suddenly a great assembly of the heavenly forces was with the angel praising God. They *said*, 'Glory to God in heaven'" (Luke 2:13-14a CEB, emphasis mine). The angels, or "heavenly forces," were praising and saying. "Praising," or *aineo*, means "speaking of the excellence of God." Much like God speaking creation into existence and calling it good, the angels continue to celebrate God's goodness at this foretaste of a new creation.

- Point out that Luke uses the word *aineo* only a few times in his Gospel, and read aloud the following verses:

The shepherds returned, glorifying and praising [aineo] God for all they had heard and seen, as it had been told them."

(Luke 2:20)

Now as he was approaching the path down from the Mount of Olives, the whole multitude of the disciples began to praise [aineo] God joyfully with a loud voice for all the deeds of power they had seen, saying,

> *'Blessed is the king*
> *who comes in the name of the Lord!*
> *Peace in heaven,*
> *and glory in the highest heaven!'"*

(Luke 19:37-38)

And they worshiped him and returned to Jerusalem with great joy, and they were continually in the temple blessing [aineo] God.

(Luke 24:52-53)

- When, where, and how does praise ring out in these scenes? What insights do you gain from comparing these instances of verbal praise?
- How is it that you communicate the "excellence of God" in your faith community? How does praise look different this time of year?

Majoring in a Minor Key

Read aloud or summarize for the group:

When the shepherds had told the Holy Family all that they had heard, Mary "treasured all these words and pondered them in her heart" (Luke 2:19). She isn't apathetic to the shepherds' excitement, but her quiet strength to treasure and ponder reminds us that sometimes Christmas is much too loud. When things aren't going according to plan, or if the holidays bring up difficult memories, our praising can feel shallow, disingenuous, or even like a wounding experience. When there is no peace in our praise, even the softest of sounds feel like a clanging, dissonant cymbal.

- What can we learn from Mary's unapologetic willingness to rest in a quiet moment and listen to her heart? What do you believe Mary might have been pondering? What helps you to sit in the silence and listen? What makes this difficult for you?
- Have you ever felt you were in a liminal space, like Mary—a thin space that seemed to be saturated with the sacred? If so, share briefly.
- Have someone read aloud Luke 2:29-32. We aren't told how Mary reacted to Simeon's prophecy, but we do know she was already well-acquainted with the interplay between awe and anguish. How do we see both wonder and pain in the story of Jesus's arrival?
- How can Christmas be a time of both awe and anguish for us today? When has Christmas been too loud or painful for you? What helps you to hold the tension of those opposites?

Singing a New Song

Read aloud or summarize for the group:

One of the prophesies typically read during the Advent season reads:

The things announced in the past—look—they've already happened,
> *but I'm declaring new things.*
> *Before they even appear,*
> *I tell you about them.*

Sing to the LORD a new song!
> *Sing his praise from the ends of the earth!*
>> *(Isaiah 42:9-10a CEB)*

Past things have "already happened" and new things are on the horizon; and yet, like Mary, somehow we can feel caught in the middle of those two truths. Singing a new song isn't easy. Sometimes a new song brings with it a dissonance that is unacceptable to those who have memorized the old song. Both magnificence and suffering ring true, but they aren't dissonant; rather, they are leading. Like a leading tone in music that leads us to finding home, or the root of the key, the dissonance of Christ's holy melody pushes us where we need to be. Sometimes we stay in the tension of the leading tone because we just aren't ready to sing ourselves home.

- Review the explanation of a leading tone in music (pages 58–60 in *Experiencing Christmas*) and discuss how it sheds light on the tensions found in the person and story of Jesus.
- What does it mean to say that peace isn't passive? When in your own experience has peace been a hard-fought reality reachable only through unspeakable lament?
- How has holy silence helped you make room for a new song?

Read aloud or summarize for the group:

Words alone cannot contain God's abundance Jesus revealed to the world. We sing, we dance, we celebrate, we treasure, we ponder, and sometimes we remain silent.

- When have you found words insufficient for expressing God's abundance revealed in Jesus?
- What activities help you celebrate God's abundance in Jesus? How are singing, dancing, celebrating, treasuring, pondering, and sitting in silence a part of your Advent and Christmas? Which of these would you like to practice more intentionally this season?

31

CLOSING ACTIVITY AND PRAYER

Again this week you will end the session by lighting candles on an Advent wreath and reading aloud Luke's account of the Christmas story, focusing your attention on one of the five senses.

Turn off the overhead lights and ask a group member to light the first and second Advent candles as participants watch in silence. Then have participants close their eyes and listen as you read the Scripture aloud slowly. Invite them to enter into the story using their imagination, becoming a participant in the scene and focusing primarily on *what they hear*. Explain that using our God-given gift of imagination in this way brings the Scripture alive for us so that we may actually encounter God and experience God's goodness and love, not just know about God. Begin with a prayer, asking God to give each of you the grace to hear, trusting that the Holy Spirit is leading your imagination.

Read the account *slowly*, allowing brief pauses where indicated:

> *In those days a decree went out from Caesar Augustus that all the world should be registered. This was the first registration and was taken while Quirinius was governor of Syria. All went to their own towns to be registered. Joseph also went from the town of Nazareth in Galilee to Judea, to the city of David called Bethlehem, because he was descended from the house and family of David. He went to be registered with Mary, to whom he was engaged and who was expecting a child.*
>
> *(Luke 2:1-5)*

Say: *Notice what you* hear *as you enter into this part of the story.* (Pause about 15 seconds.)

> *While they were there, the time came for her to deliver her child. And she gave birth to her firstborn son and wrapped him in bands of cloth and laid him in a manger, because there was no place in the guest room.*
>
> *(Luke 2:6-7)*

Say: *Notice what you* hear *as you enter into this part of the story.* (Pause about 15 seconds.)

> *Now in that same region there were shepherds living in the fields, keeping watch over their flock by night. Then an angel of the Lord stood before them, and the glory of the Lord shone around them, and they were terrified. But the angel said to them, "Do not be afraid, for see, I am bringing you good news of great joy for all the people: to you is born this day in the city of David a Savior, who is the Messiah, the Lord. This will be a sign for you: you will find a child wrapped in bands of cloth and lying in a manger." And suddenly there was with the angel a multitude of the heavenly host, praising God and saying,*
>
> > *"Glory to God in the highest heaven,*
> > *and on earth peace among those whom he favors!"*
> >
> > *(Luke 2:8-14)*

Say: *Notice what you* hear *as you enter into this part of the story.* (Pause about 15 seconds.)

> *When the angels had left them and gone into heaven, the shepherds said to one another, "Let us go now to Bethlehem and see this thing that has taken place, which the Lord has made known to us." So they went with haste and found Mary and Joseph and the child lying in the manger. When they saw this, they made known what had been told them about this child, and all who heard it were amazed at what the shepherds told them, and Mary treasured all these words and pondered them in her heart.*
>
> > *(Luke 2:15-19)*

Say: *Notice what you* hear *as you enter into this part of the story.* (Pause about 15 seconds.)

> *The shepherds returned, glorifying and praising God for all they had heard and seen, just as it had been told them.*
>
> > *(Luke 2:20)*

33

Say: *Notice what you* hear *as you enter into this part of the story.* (Pause about 15 seconds.)

Invite participants to slowly return to the room and open their eyes when they are ready. Then move into a time of brief sharing.

Discuss:

- What did you notice as you entered the story, focusing on *what you heard?* What stood out to you and why?

Closing Prayer

God of all good gifts, the announcement of Christ's birth is such good news that we want to rejoice and offer you praise. Thank you for the beautiful and joyful sounds of this season. We acknowledge there also are times when these sounds seem more like noise and praise is more challenging, especially if we're dealing with difficult memories or painful experiences. Help us to be like Mary, holding the tension of both wonder and pain, joy and sadness. In the midst of all the activity, may we carve out some space to sit in silence, listen for your voice, and receive your love. Give us a new song of praise this Advent. Amen.

ADDITIONAL OPTIONS FOR GROUP ACTIVITIES

If your group is able to meet for longer than 60 minutes, consider adding one or both of the following activities that invite participants to experience the meaning of the season through their *hearing*:

- **Sing one or two Christmas carols together**—In advance, poll the group for favorite Christmas carols and choose several to sing together. Play recorded instrumental versions of the carols or have a group member provide accompaniment by playing guitar or a portable keyboard. Or if you like, make a joyful noise without accompaniment!

- **Have a time of silence**—Invite participants to deepen their breathing, signaling to their minds and bodies that they are slowing down. Ask them to become aware of God's presence, which is as close as their breath—all around them and within them. Then invite them to simply rest in God's loving presence, just as they would sit silently with someone they love—someone whose loving presence requires no words. If their minds wander, they may simply notice their thoughts without judgment and release them, watching them float away like clouds in the sky. Or if they prefer, they may ponder God's goodness and listen for God's voice. Set a timer on your phone for 2-3 minutes (or longer if desired, depending on your group; you might choose to set the alarm to chimes). After the silence, invite participants to share what the experience was like for them.

- **Optional discussion:**
  ◊ How does Mary's silent pondering show us the value of silence in our own lives?
  ◊ How does silence point to the mystery of the Incarnation?

SESSION THREE

DO YOU TASTE
WHAT I TASTE?

PLANNING THE SESSION

Session Goals

Through this session's discussion and activities, participants will be encouraged to:

- Reflect on the human details of the Christmas story that sometimes make us uncomfortable.
- Recognize that Mary offered her body as nourishment to the one who later would offer his body for our nourishment.
- Consider the ways that Christmas is about vulnerability, intimacy, and humility.
- Explore the different "flavors" of the Gospels and the pictures they reveal of Jesus.

36

- Consider how eating is meant to be a communal activity that brings us together with others.
- Give ourselves permission to slow down and allow room in our souls for desire.

Biblical Foundation

- Psalm 34:8
- Matthew 1:1
- Mark 1:1
- Luke 1:4; 2:7
- John 1:1
- Philippians 2:5-11

Preparation

- Read chapter 3, "Do You Taste What I Taste?" in Matt Rawle's *Experiencing Christmas*.
- Read through this Leader Guide session in its entirety to familiarize yourself with the material being covered.
- Read and reflect on the Biblical Foundation passages listed above.
- Plan to have extra Bibles on hand for participants.
- You will want to have your DVD player or computer ready to watch the video segment.
- You also might have a markerboard or large sheet of paper available for recording group members' ideas and paper and pens for note taking, if desired.
- Place several food-scented holiday candles in the room (for example, cinnamon, sugar cookie, or gingerbread) and burn them for the duration of the class session, filling the room with an inviting aroma. (Use multiple candles of the same scent and be sure to check with group members in advance for any sensitivities.)

- Provide Christmas goodies for snacking, if desired. (Omit this if you are doing the first idea under "Additional Options for Group Activities.")
- Have an Advent wreath, candles, and lighter available for the Closing Activity.
- If you will be doing the activities under "Additional Options for Group Activity," read through those options thoroughly and gather any items needed for that time together.

OPENING ACTIVITY AND PRAYER

Welcome participants as they arrive. When most are present, ask each group member to respond briefly to the following question, writing responses on a markerboard or large sheet of paper, if desired.

- What is your favorite dish, goodie, or drink to taste at Christmas?

Read aloud or summarize for the group:

> The sights and sounds of the season are everywhere, but taste is underrated. Taste can offer a sense of wonder or the comfort of home. Taste is a gift. The simple joy of tasting something delicious causes us involuntarily to stop, breathe, and be thankful. Today we will be exploring how our sense of taste—and its related sense, smell—can enrich our experience and understanding of God's love this Christmas. Let's open in prayer.

Opening Prayer

Dear Lord, thank you for this time to feast upon your word. We pray that during this season of Advent you would continue to enrich our experience of Christmas so that we might rediscover the meaning of the season. May our sense of taste—and its related sense, smell—become signs for us, pointing us to the Incarnation so that we might experience your love in a new way today. We long to taste your goodness! In Jesus's name. Amen.

WATCH DVD SEGMENT

Play session 3: "Do You Taste What I Taste?" on the *Experiencing Christmas* DVD or via Amplify Media.
Discuss:

- Did anything specific stand out as you watched the video?
- What is something you learned or experienced that seems new or *renewed*?

Invite the group to keep both the video and the book in mind throughout the discussion.

STUDY AND DISCUSSION

The First Communion

Read aloud or summarize for the group:

> Between angels, shepherds, livestock, and all the hubbub that the Gospels record about Jesus's birth, at some point Mary nursed Jesus. The Gospels say nothing about what I assume to be a holy and intimate connection between mother and child. I'm not surprised that this detail is overlooked. Scripture unfortunately glosses over the whole event.... Could it be with all the divine images of dreams and angels, shepherds and stars, that the actual birth seems far too human to report? Perhaps the male authors of the Gospels didn't know what to say, or they were too entrenched in their own perspective to recognize the omission.

- Have someone read aloud Luke 2:7 and Matthew 1:18; 2:1a. Why do you think the Gospel writers did not include details related to Jesus's birth? What are the details you wish had been recorded—the things you wonder about?

- Do you agree that we Christians seem to have an easier time accepting Jesus's divinity while the human parts tend to make us uncomfortable? Why or why not?

Read aloud or summarize for the group:

> [At some point] Mary offered Jesus his first meal. The vulnerability and intimacy of that moment just might have had the power to bring creation to its knees in praise and thanksgiving. It's a holy moment that, in a way, looks forward to the Last Supper. Mary offered her body as nourishment to the One who, some thirty years later, would offer his body for ours in the breaking of the bread. From the beginning of Jesus's life there has been a holy reciprocity of food in the most divine and intimate sense.

- According to the author, why were icons of Mary nursing Jesus a tradition in the church until the sixteenth century? What does the comparison of Mary's nourishment of Christ and Christ's nourishment of us through Holy Communion offer us? How does it speak to you?
- How does the image of Jesus's first meal open you to the vulnerability and intimacy of Christmas? What do the vulnerability and intimacy of Christmas reveal to us about God's love?

Different Flavors

Read aloud or summarize for the group:

> The Christmas story reminds us to take a moment and consider someone else's perspective. Or maybe more accurately, to recognize the voices that have been overlooked, forgotten, or silenced. In Matthew's Gospel we

40

receive an inner glance into Joseph's experience of Jesus's birth. Mary doesn't ever speak. Conversely, Luke offers us great detail on Mary's experience, and Joseph never speaks. One Gospel remembers magi; another Gospel records shepherds. In one Gospel the family is already in Bethlehem, and in the other they travel for the census. The stories are true, and they disagree on the details.

- Referring to Matthew 1–2 and Luke 1–2, discuss some of the differences found in these Gospel accounts of the Christmas story.

- Do you find these differences to be causes of confusion or curiosity? How can these differences enhance our understanding and experience of Christmas?

Read aloud or summarize for the group:

Matthew, Mark, Luke, and John all offer us different angles, different perspectives, and different flavors of the one we call Christ, the Lord. The way each Gospel begins gives us the flavor of what's to come....

When we read the Gospels together, comparing and contrasting the different flavors of the story, we aren't building something new and independent from the sources; rather we experience a fuller picture of both the individual Gospel and how the Gospel contributes to the overall picture of Jesus...

When reading Scripture patiently, letting the different flavors dance with and against each other, we finally begin to understand Scripture's depth; and what a feast it is!

- Read aloud Matthew 1:1, Mark 1:1, Luke 1:1-4, and John 1:1. What do these opening lines of the Gospels reveal to us about the picture of Jesus each writer is presenting?

- How do the four Gospels offer us different "flavors" of the banquet that is Jesus? Based on the author's comments on the Gospels (pages 78–79 in *Experiencing Christmas*), how would you describe each of those flavors? (Example: Matthew—sacrificial King; Mark—mysterious miracle worker; Luke—redeemer of outcasts; John—the Word of God)
- How do the four Gospels give us a fuller picture of the Gospel story and the overall picture of Jesus?

Double-Boiling Chocolate

Read aloud or summarize for the group:

Even before the Gospels were penned, between something like AD 70-110, Paul presents us with who this Messiah is in Philippians 2:5-11—the oldest, formal worshipful picture of Jesus called the "Christ Hymn." Here in this "Christ Hymn" there is a word about creation, claiming that Jesus is of the same substance as God, and then immediately there is a humbling. Christ is of the same divine substance, but not as a means of exploitation. Christ emptied the divine self for everything that wasn't Christ. This emptying and humility has huge implications for what we understand about God's love.

- What does the humble emptying of Christ teach us about God's love? about Christmas?
- How did God have to rely on humanity in order to save it? What does this reveal to us about God's faithfulness toward us?

It's Never a Table for One

Read aloud or summarize for the group:

When we see Jesus eating in the Gospels, it is always with someone. Maybe that's the real lesson here, that eating is a communal activity.

- To what degree is eating a communal activity for you? Who in your circle needs to know they have a place at your table and in your life?
- What is the difference between an "eat to live" and a "live to eat" attitude? What do you prioritize more often: quick meals catered to you and your schedule, or table fellowship? Why?

Read aloud or summarize for the group:

> Scripture doesn't really tell us what Jesus ate. We know that Jesus ate the Passover meal, and Jesus ate bread and fish, but outside of that, Scripture really doesn't detail what Jesus ate. We can assume that Jesus ate Mediterranean food. It's fascinating to think that Jesus probably ate lamb and grape leaves and probably hummus, and it all seems beautifully mundane.

- What do you imagine could have been Jesus's favorite food? his least favorite?
- If Jesus came to you today and asked you to join him for dinner, how would you respond? Where would you want to eat with Jesus—your kitchen, a five-star restaurant, a food truck, somewhere else?
- What were mealtimes like in your childhood household? What are mealtimes like for you now? How might mealtime be different if you saw it as an invitation to be present to Jesus through the food and company in front of you?
- What opportunities do you have in your family, congregation, or community to come together around food?

Read aloud or summarize for the group:

> Cooking takes time, and it's supposed to. When we slow down, when we become vulnerable by waiting, we are making room in our souls for desire.... The beautiful thing about Advent is that we are given permission to do the

same thing, to slow down, to waste time, to allow room in our souls for desire, to sit and waste time with an old friend, to again feel the desire of friendship, to sit and waste time with your spouse, to again feel the desire within marriage, to sit and waste time with your siblings, to feel the desire of family, to sit in the sanctuary, staring at the Advent wreath, getting lost in the chrismon tree, kneeling at the table, in order to be filled with the desire to see the radiant beams of the Christ Child's holy face.

- How does slowing down and waiting make us vulnerable? How does it make room in our souls for desire? When and how have you experienced this?
- How does Advent give us permission to make room in our souls for desire? What kinds of desires are you making room for in your soul this Advent?

Read aloud or summarize for the group:

Food is a vehicle through which we connect with our history, our friends, and even our enemies. Over and over again we have stories of Jesus eating with people. He eats with sinners; he eats with saints. He was labeled a glutton and a drunkard. His disciples picked grain on the Sabbath. He fed thousands with almost nothing, identified himself as the bread from heaven, and took that same bread, broke it, gave it holy significance as his body, and offers it to us. From farm to table, no one truly eats alone, and I think that first Christmas taught us this all along.

When we gather around the Lord's Table, we remember and celebrate that Jesus offers his body as nourishment.

- What can we learn about food and table fellowship from Jesus's example? How might food and mealtimes help you to connect with your history, your friends, and even your enemies?
- In what way is it true that "no one really eats alone"?

- Read aloud Psalm 34:8. What does this verse mean? When and how do we "taste" the Lord's goodness? How is Holy Communion an invitation to "taste and see that the Lord is good"?

CLOSING ACTIVITY AND PRAYER

As you have done in previous weeks, end the session by lighting candles on an Advent wreath and reading aloud Luke's account of the Christmas story, focusing your attention on one of the five senses.

Turn off the overhead lights and ask a group member to light the first, second, and third Advent candles as participants watch in silence. Then have participants close their eyes and listen as you read the Scripture aloud slowly. Invite them to enter into the story using their imagination, becoming a participant in the scene and focusing primarily on *what they smell*. Explain that using our God-given gift of imagination in this way brings the Scripture alive for us so that we may actually encounter God and experience God's goodness and love, not just know about God. Begin with a prayer, asking God to give each of you the grace to imagine the scents in the story, trusting that the Holy Spirit is leading your imagination.

Read the account *slowly*, allowing brief pauses where indicated:

> In those days a decree went out from Caesar Augustus that all the world should be registered. This was the first registration and was taken while Quirinius was governor of Syria. All went to their own towns to be registered. Joseph also went from the town of Nazareth in Galilee to Judea, to the city of David called Bethlehem, because he was descended from the house and family of David. He went to be registered with Mary, to whom he was engaged and who was expecting a child.
>
> *(Luke 2:1-5)*

45

Say: *Notice any scents you might detect as you enter into this part of the story.* (Pause about 15 seconds.)

> *While they were there, the time came for her to deliver her child. And she gave birth to her firstborn son and wrapped him in bands of cloth and laid him in a manger, because there was no place in the guest room.*
>
> *(Luke 2:6-7)*

Say: *Notice any scents you might detect as you enter into this part of the story.* (Pause about 15 seconds.) *Now I invite you to imagine the moments following Jesus's birth as Mary and Joseph welcomed their newborn son and attended to his needs, including Mary offering Jesus his first meal. Notice whatever stands out to you.* (Pause another 15 seconds.)

> *Now in that same region there were shepherds living in the fields, keeping watch over their flock by night. Then an angel of the Lord stood before them, and the glory of the Lord shone around them, and they were terrified. But the angel said to them, "Do not be afraid, for see, I am bringing you good news of great joy for all the people: to you is born this day in the city of David a Savior, who is the Messiah, the Lord. This will be a sign for you: you will find a child wrapped in bands of cloth and lying in a manger." And suddenly there was with the angel a multitude of the heavenly host, praising God and saying,*
>
> > *"Glory to God in the highest heaven,*
> > *and on earth peace among those whom he favors!"*
> >
> > *(Luke 2:8-14)*

Say: *Notice any scents you might detect as you enter into this part of the story.* (Pause about 15 seconds.)

> *When the angels had left them and gone into heaven, the shepherds said to one another, "Let us go now to Bethlehem and see this thing that has taken place, which the Lord has made known to us." So they went with haste and found Mary*

and Joseph and the child lying in the manger. When they saw this, they made known what had been told them about this child, and all who heard it were amazed at what the shepherds told them, and Mary treasured all these words and pondered them in her heart.

(Luke 2:15-19)

Say: *Notice any* scents *you might detect as you enter into this part of the story.* (Pause about 15 seconds.)

The shepherds returned, glorifying and praising God for all they had heard and seen, just as it had been told them.

(Luke 2:20)

Say: *Notice any* scents *you might detect as you enter into this part of the story.* (Pause about 15 seconds.)

Invite participants to slowly return to the room and open their eyes when they are ready. Then move into a time of discussion.

Discuss:

- What did you notice as you entered the story, *focusing on the* scents you detected?
- What did you notice when you imagined Mary and Joseph welcoming and nurturing their infant son? What stood out to you and why?
- Savor these words: "*Mary offered her body as nourishment to the One who, some thirty years later, would offer his body for ours in the breaking of the bread.*" What nourishment do these images of love offer you today?

Closing Prayer

Lord of all desire, we praise you for the gifts of taste and smell, which remind us of your grace and goodness. Advent is an invitation to slow down and make room in our souls for desire—and to allow our hunger to lead us to you. This Advent may we taste and see that you are good, and may we celebrate your goodness and love whenever we break bread together; in Jesus's name. Amen.

ADDITIONAL OPTIONS FOR GROUP ACTIVITIES

If your group is able to meet for longer than 60 minutes, consider adding one of the following activities that invite participants to experience the meaning of the season through their *taste*.

- **Enjoy Christmas dishes or desserts**—In advance, invite everyone to bring a favorite Christmas dish or dessert to share, along with copies of the recipe. As you savor the tastes and smells of the food, talk about how these seasonal delights signify our anticipation and expectation for the coming of Jesus.

- **Share Holy Communion**—In advance, invite a pastor to consecrate elements and preside at a closing celebration of Holy Communion. Use "A Service of Word and Table" from *The United Methodist Hymnal* or the Communion liturgy for your denomination.

SESSION 4

Do You Feel What I Feel?

Planning the Session

Session Goals

Through this session's discussion and activities, participants will be encouraged to:

- Recognize the essential nature of our sense of touch.
- Explore the benefits of healthy touch.
- Acknowledge that unwanted touch can cause incredible harm and consider ways to avoid harmful touch.
- Consider what we learn about God through stories where Jesus used the power of touch for healing.
- Understand that sometimes good touch means knowing when to let go.

- Consider how the Incarnation has changed everything, enabling us to see hope, hear peace, taste love, and feel joy.

Biblical Foundation

- Luke 2:1-12
- Luke 7:11-17
- Luke 7:36-50
- Luke 8:46-48
- Luke 2:28-32
- Luke 23:50-53
- John 20:17-18
- Isaiah 40:1-2

Preparation

- Read chapter 4, "Do You Feel What I Feel?" in Matt Rawle's *Experiencing Christmas*.
- Read through this Leader Guide session in its entirety to familiarize yourself with the material being covered.
- Read and reflect on the Biblical Foundation passages listed above.
- Plan to have extra Bibles on hand for participants.
- You will want to have your DVD player or computer ready to watch the video segment.
- You also might have a markerboard or large sheet of paper available for recording group members' ideas and paper and pens for note taking, if desired.
- Have an Advent wreath, candles, and lighter available for the Closing Activity.
- If you will be doing the activities under "Additional Options for Group Activity," read through those options thoroughly and gather any items needed for that time together.

OPENING ACTIVITY AND PRAYER

Welcome participants as they arrive. When most are present, ask each group member to respond briefly to the following questions, writing responses on a markerboard or large sheet of paper, if desired.

- On a typical day, what things do you touch most often? How often do you experience human touch each day?

Read aloud or summarize for the group:

> We can navigate the world without sight—it's difficult but possible. Many people can live quite well without a sense of hearing. COVID-19 taught many of us that, even though it's a drag, we can live without taste. We cannot live without touch. It would be impossible. We must be able to feel the world around us. Touch is the most profound of all the senses that God assumed through Christ, and Christmas is a time to celebrate the full meaning of the Incarnation. Today, we will be exploring what touch has to teach us about God's love in Christ.

Opening Prayer

Immanuel, thank you for putting on flesh and becoming one of us. In this final session of our study, enrich our experience of Christmas once again so that we might rediscover the meaning of the season. May our sense of touch become a sign for us, pointing us to the Incarnation so that we might experience your love in a new way today. We long to feel your goodness; in Jesus's name. Amen.

WATCH DVD SEGMENT

Play Session 4: "Do You Feel What I Feel?" on the *Experiencing Christmas* DVD or via Amplify Media.

Discuss:

- · Did anything specific stand out as you watched the video?
- What is something you learned or experienced that seems new or *renewed*?

Invite the group to keep both the video and the book in mind throughout the discussion.

STUDY AND DISCUSSION

The Power of Touch

Read aloud or summarize for the group:

> Good, healthy touch protects us. That protection might initially be painful, but a painful touch might end up saving you from a lot of trouble. Touch also helps communicate comfort and love. However, touch needs permission. Touch is so powerful that, if used inappropriately, it can cause incredible harm that takes a lifetime to heal.

Discuss:

- When has touch helped to protect you, even if painful at first—such as touching a hot stove, sensing a pit in your stomach, or feeling the hair on the back of your neck stand up? What would it be like to live in the world without this protective benefit of touch?
- How might we define "good, healthy touch"? How has good, healthy touch comforted, encouraged, or communicated love to you recently?
- Why is it important for touch to have permission, and what might that look like in everyday life (consider home, school, work, church, and community life)?
- How does unwanted or inappropriate touch cause harm? How can we do better at addressing the wounds of those who have been harmed by unwanted touch—especially as the church?

- Where do you fall on the touch spectrum? In terms of healthy touch, are you generally open to it, indifferent to it, or resistant to it—especially from people you do not know well? How big is your personal bubble?

Read aloud or summarize for the group:

During Advent we prepare for the Incarnation—God entering into time and creation and assuming our humanity. Jesus experienced what it is like to be full and to be empty, to stretch and to skin a knee. This fully divine and fully human Jesus certainly had growing pains and experienced the confusion of puberty, the headaches of dehydration, and the joy of a friend's embrace.

Discuss:

- The Incarnation is a profound mystery. When you consider that God put on flesh and became like us, what does this say to you about God? What does it say about human life and the kind of relationship we can have with God?
- What are some of the everyday ways that Jesus would have experienced life through the sense of touch? Write them on a board or large sheet of paper. As you look at the list, what stands out or strikes you most, and why?

Read aloud or summarize for the group:

Jesus also used the power of touch for healing. He drew close to those who were overlooked or outcast in society— the sick, the diseased, and the unclean—yet he did not recoil from their touch. His acceptance of their touch was the beginning of a journey of healing.

Discuss:

- Read aloud or summarize the healing stories found in Luke 7:11-17, 7:36-50, and 8:46-48. How did touch bring healing in each instance? What customs or beliefs did Jesus challenge in these instances? What do we learn about God through these stories?

- How have you experienced or witnessed Jesus's healing touch in your own life and/or the lives of those you love?
- How might you offer healing touch to those around you?

Read aloud or summarize for the group:

There are only two times that the Gospels recall Jesus being fully embraced. He was fully embraced at his infancy (Luke 2:28-32), and he was fully embraced at his death (Luke 23:50-53). Luke seems to communicate that to fully embrace Christ, we are to take hold of the entire story.

Discuss:

- Read aloud Luke 2:28-32. What did Simeon's full embrace of Jesus announce about salvation?
- Now read aloud Luke 23:50-53. According to these verses, what is that salvation?

Read aloud or summarize for the group:

The Resurrection account in John's Gospel reminds us that good touch is not always about holding on. Sometimes it means knowing when to let go. When Mary recognizes the risen Christ on that first Easter Sunday morning, he tells her not to hold on to him. Scholars have different ideas about this strange prohibition.

Discuss:

- Read aloud John 20:17. What are some possible reasons Jesus asked Mary not to hold on to him? Which resonates most with you?

- How does holding loosely to the past allow us to live into the reality of God's bigger story? How have you experienced this in your own life?

A Sense-able God

Read aloud or summarize for the group:

> Everything feels different this time of year because *all of creation, with intent or accident, recognizes that when God put on flesh, everything changed.* Because of the Incarnation, God knows what it means to embrace and what it means to be held. God knows the power and responsibility of touch and the pain of crucifixion. Hands that reached out for his mother grew into hands outstretched revealing the vulnerable and passionate love God has for all of creation. Even touch seems different this time of year—the embrace of family who've been away for far too long, the choosing and wrapping of packages for excited friends, waxy fingers holding a tiny candle during "Silent Night." Everything feels different this time of year because *everything changed when God came to walk among us.*

- What do you enjoy touching or feeling at Christmas—the chill in the air, the sharpness of evergreen needles, the embrace of loved ones, beautiful presents, something else? How does the sense of touch heighten your experience of Christmas?
- Imagine Jesus asking you, "Do you feel what I feel?" What do you sense Jesus inviting you to feel this Christmas? What might it mean for you to follow Jesus and partner with him to change the world?

In Those Days... On This Day... You Will See

Read aloud or summarize for the group:

> The beginning of Luke's Nativity is proclaimed in past tense. "In those days" *was* the first registration. Joseph

went to Bethlehem because he was a descendant of David. Joseph *was* engaged to Mary, she *was* expecting a child, and there *was* no room for them in the guestroom. The entire saga from the palace to the manger is written in the past tense. This might not seem important until the heavens open up and the angels appear saying, "Don't be afraid! Look! I bring good news to you—wonderful, joyous news for all people. Your savior *is born today* in David's city. He is Christ the Lord" (Luke 2:10-11 CEB, emphasis added)....

The angel continues and offers the shepherds a future trajectory—"This *is* a sign for you: you *will* find a newborn baby wrapped snugly and lying in a manger" (Luke 2:12 CEB, empasis added). It is definitive. There is no room for maybe in this new, inbreaking creation.... "In those days" gives way for "Today," so that all our days will know the salvation offered through Jesus's defeat of death.

Discuss:

- How do the verb tenses in Luke 2:1-12 help us to see the inbreaking of God's new creation through Christ?
- How has Christ's coming forever changed the ways that we see, hear, taste, touch, and smell? How has your own perception and experience of the world—the ways that you see, hear, taste, touch, and smell—been changed because of Christ?

God Is with Us

Read aloud or summarize for the group:

The light of hope, the sound of peace, a taste of love, and finally a touch of joy. Joy is the steadfast assurance that God is with us.... Joy is the touch of the divine for which our Advent expectation has been building. With each passing week of preparation, the divine comes increasingly closer to us until God becomes one of us. God enters creation in a forever-present presence so that we might see hope, hear peace, taste love, and feel joy.

Discuss:

- How has your experience of Advent been different this year? How have your senses helped you to experience the meaning of Christmas and God's love in new ways?
- Share an example of a way you have experienced each of the following this Advent: the light of hope, the sound of peace, the taste of love, the touch of joy.
- How is God inviting you to share in God's vision of salvation for the world?

Closing Activity and Prayer

As you have done each week of our study, end the session by lighting candles on an Advent wreath and reading aloud Luke's account of the Christmas story, focusing your attention on one of the five senses.

Turn off the overhead lights and ask a group member to light all four Advent candles as participants watch in silence. Then have participants close their eyes and listen as you read the Scripture aloud slowly. Invite them to enter into the story using their imagination, becoming a participant in the scene and focusing primarily on *what they can touch or feel*. Explain that using our God-given gift of imagination in this way brings the Scripture alive for us so that we may actually encounter God and experience God's goodness and love, not just know about God. Begin with a prayer, asking God to give each of you the grace to feel, trusting that the Holy Spirit is leading your imagination. Read the account *slowly*, allowing brief pauses where indicated:

> *In those days a decree went out from Caesar Augustus that all the world should be registered. This was the first registration and was taken while Quirinius was governor of Syria. All went to their own towns to be registered. Joseph also went from the town of Nazareth in Galilee to Judea, to the city of David called Bethlehem, because he was descended from the house*

and family of David. He went to be registered with Mary, to whom he was engaged and who was expecting a child.

(Luke 2:1-5)

Say: *Notice what you can* touch or feel *as you enter into this part of the story.* (Pause about 15 seconds.)

While they were there, the time came for her to deliver her child. And she gave birth to her firstborn son and wrapped him in bands of cloth and laid him in a manger, because there was no place in the guest room.

(Luke 2:6-7)

Say: *Notice what you can* touch or feel *as you enter into this part of the story.* (Pause about 15 seconds.)

Now in that same region there were shepherds living in the fields, keeping watch over their flock by night. Then an angel of the Lord stood before them, and the glory of the Lord shone around them, and they were terrified. But the angel said to them, "Do not be afraid, for see, I am bringing you good news of great joy for all the people: to you is born this day in the city of David a Savior, who is the Messiah, the Lord. This will be a sign for you: you will find a child wrapped in bands of cloth and lying in a manger." And suddenly there was with the angel a multitude of the heavenly host, praising God and saying,

"Glory to God in the highest heaven,
and on earth peace among those whom he favors!"

(Luke 2:8-14)

Say: *Notice what you can* touch or feel *as you enter into this part of the story.* (Pause about 15 seconds.)

When the angels had left them and gone into heaven, the shepherds said to one another, "Let us go now to Bethlehem and see this thing that has taken place, which the Lord has made known to us." So they went with haste and found Mary and Joseph and the child lying in the manger. When they saw this, they made known what had been told them about this child, and all who heard it were amazed at what the shepherds told them, and Mary treasured all these words and pondered them in her heart.

(Luke 2:15-19)

Say: *Notice what you can* touch or feel *as you enter into this part of the story.* (Pause about 15 seconds.)

The shepherds returned, glorifying and praising God for all they had heard and seen, just as it had been told them.

(Luke 2:20)

Say: *Notice what you can* touch or feel *as you enter into this part of the story.* (Pause about 15 seconds.)

Invite participants to slowly return to the room and open their eyes when they are ready. Then move into a time of discussion.

Discuss:

- What did you notice as you entered the story, focusing on what you could touch or feel? What stood out to you and why?

Closing Prayer

Almighty God, when you put on flesh, everything changed! When you assumed our humanity in Jesus, you adopted our senses—seeing with divine eyes, hearing with holy ears, tasting with nurturing love, and touching with healing hands. As we have been experiencing Christmas through our senses during the weeks of Advent, we have rediscovered the wondrous gift of the Incarnation and the unlimited depths of your love. We have been reminded that you came not only to take part in our story but to redeem it—to redeem all of us and invite us to follow you. That is our Christmas wish, Lord—to follow you with an ever-increasing awareness of your loving presence so that we might always see hope, hear peace, taste love, and feel love; in Jesus's name we pray. Amen.

ADDITIONAL OPTIONS
FOR GROUP ACTIVITIES

If your group is able to meet for longer than 60 minutes, consider adding one or both of the following activities that invite participants to experience the meaning of the season through their *touch*:

- **Wrap presents for Angel Tree recipients**—Select several names from an Angel Tree sponsored by your church or another community organization, or adopt a family in your community. Invite group members to purchase gifts and bring them to this session—along with wrapping paper, ribbon, bows, and tape. Play Christmas music as you enjoy wrapping the presents together.

- **Pass the Peace**—Invite participants to pass the peace to one another while honoring one another's personal space preferences. As group members greet one another, they may ask, "Would you like a blessing or word of encouragement only, a blessing with a touch on the back or shoulder, or an embrace?" Let this be a time of offering safe, healthy, healing touch. (*Note*: Let group members know that if anyone is uncomfortable participating in this exercise for any reason, they may excuse themselves without judgment. Be sure to extend compassion to all who may wrestle with expressions of touch.)

- **Have a time of silent prayer with gentle touch**—Invite participants to sit in a circle. As leader, get up and stand behind the person to your right. As you gently place a hand on the person's back or shoulder, pray briefly for that person silently. Then move to the next person to the right and do the same. As you move to the third person, the first person you prayed for stands up and moves to stand behind the person to their right (the person between you), placing a hand on the person's back or shoulder and praying briefly for them silently. Continue in this fashion, moving around the circle until everyone has been prayed for and has prayed in turn for everyone in the group.

- **Optional discussion:**
  ◊ What was this experience like for you? How did the combination of silent prayer and gentle touch bring comfort, peace, or healing?

WATCH VIDEOS BASED ON *EXPERIENCING CHRISTMAS: CHRIST IN THE SIGHTS AND SOUNDS OF ADVENT* WITH MATT RAWLE THROUGH AMPLIFY MEDIA.

www.ingramcontent.com/pod-product-compliance
Lightning Source LLC
Chambersburg PA
CBHW010858090426
42737CB00020B/3418